T0131749

SAMMY'S BIG MISTAKE

THE DAY I DIDN'T FEEL LOVABLE

Written by Samuel "Sammy" Deutscher
Illustrated by Tina C. Wood

AuthorHouse™
1663 Liberty Drive
Bloomington, IN 47403
www.authorhouse.com
Phone: 833-262-8899

Because of the dynamic nature of the Internet, any web addresses or links contained
in this book may have changed since publication and may no longer be valid. The views
expressed in this work are solely those of the author and do not necessarily reflect the
views of the publisher, and the publisher hereby disclaims any responsibility for them.

Any people depicted in stock imagery provided by Getty Images are models,
and such images are being used for illustrative purposes only.
Certain stock imagery © Getty Images.

This book is printed on acid-free paper.

ISBN: 978-1-6655-7561-4 (sc)
ISBN: 978-1-6655-7560-7 (e)

Library of Congress Control Number: 2022920980

Print information available on the last page.

Published by AuthorHouse 12/02/2022

authorHOUSE

Hi! My name is Sammy, and I'm going to tell you about my first days of kindergarten. It should have been fun, but it wasn't. I made a *big* mistake!

The night before school, my father told me my Hebrew name. He said, "Your name is Shlomo. You'd better remember it for tomorrow!"

I didn't know what dad was talking about, but I would try to remember what he said.

The house was already quiet for the night. Everyone was sleeping except for me. I was scared! I couldn't remember my Hebrew name.

I was nervous about my first day of school. I was trying to remember my Hebrew name, and I couldn't.

Today was the big day! I was waiting for the school bus, and I was nervous because I couldn't remember my Hebrew name.

I started to get really scared on the ride to school. What was my Hebrew name? What was going to happen in school?

I was so nervous and scared. My
mind went blank, and I said,

That night, when he heard the story, my dad was very upset with me. He said,

Shlomo? Shmooel? I felt like I was
going crazy. Shlomo? Shmooel? What
was this?

The next day, I was scared on the bus ride to school again; my dad was still upset with me. These bus rides were not fun.

I thought that not remembering my name was bad enough. This time, I really made a big mistake!

I stuck my tongue out and said a bad word. As punishment, the teacher washed my mouth out with soap and made me stand in the corner facing the wall.

I was scared on the bus ride home.
Everyone at school was upset with
me, and what were my dad and mom
going to do?

That night, my bubbe called me on the telephone. She said,

"I love you, Sammy!"

Finally, something good happened. I was lovable after all!

I was able to sleep that night. I was lovable, and I was going to apologize.

The next day, I apologized to everyone for being rude. It made me feel good to say I was sorry, and I was forgiven.

Printed in the United States
by Baker & Taylor Publisher Services